ECHOES OF MEMORY

Selected Poems of Lucio Mariani

Translated from the Italian by Anthony Molino

Wesleyan University Press Middletown, Connecticut

Published by Wesleyan University Press, Middletown, CT 06459

Translation © 2003 by Anthony Molino
Original Italian © 1995, 2001 by Lucio Mariani
Afterword © Thomas Harrison
The Italian poems of Lucio Mariani, reprinted from his books *Il torto della preda: Versi scelti, 1974–1994* (Milan: Crocetti Editore, 1995) and *Qualche notizia del tempo* (Milan: Crocetti Editore, 2001), appear courtesy of Crocetti Editore. The poem "Scacco matto" appears courtesy of Edizioni dell'Elefante (Rome, 2001).

Printed in the United States of America
Designed and set in Cycles type by Julie Allred,
B. Williams & Associates

Library of Congress Cataloging-in-Publication Data
Mariani, Lucio, 1936–
[Poems. English & Italian. Selections]
Echoes of memory : selected poems of Lucio Mariani ;
translated from the Italian by Anthony Molino.
    p. cm. — (Wesleyan poetry)
English and Italian.
ISBN 0-8195-6495-8 (alk. paper) — ISBN 0-8195-6496-6 (pbk. : alk. paper)
1. Mariani, Lucio, 1936—Translations into English.
I. Molino, Anthony, 1957– II. Title. III. Series.
PQ4873.A6948A26 2003
851'.914—dc21   2002191012

5   4   3   2   1

CONTENTS

> ... *farsi catturare viva*
> *è l'unico torto della preda.*
> Lucio Mariani, "Più voci"

"Getting captured alive / is the prey's lone mistake." These closing lines of Lucio Mariani's poem "Più voci" ("Several Voices") are also the two lines that close out his collection of selected poems, *Il torto della preda: Versi scelti, 1974-1994* (Milan: Crocetti Editore, 1995), and lend that book its title. The title is especially apt because it defines precisely what Mariani's poetry invites, dares, and defies. Like the prey confident of its cunning and agility, it is a poetry that insists on being hunted and pursued, challenging its readers' intelligence in an intriguing and seductive defiance of capture. Arguably, this is a hallmark of any poem worth its salt: for to be captured alive is, for a poem, a sign of insufficiency, of fated conception, of its "mistake." It is to render its soul to the vivisection of analysis when, as Mariani suggests in a poem entitled "Lethe," what distinguishes the birth of a "solemn verse . . . a true poem" is really a sign of immortality: "for a new immortal child has been born unto all."

A good friend to whom I showed these translations had this to say about Mariani's work: "It seems to me that there is a certain kind of poet that feels that the ancient world knew what poetry was, and perhaps should have remained. I know that begs a description, but it's a description that rests in the ancient tomes themselves—in Pausanius or Homer, say. . . . There is, of course, a 'classical sensibility' that is difficult to replicate these days, without seeming like a nostalgia artist or a parodic writer. Peter Handke, it strikes me, was one good hand at this style, which I took to be modeled after Vergil's *Georgics*. Now there's Lucio Mariani's work." It would be a mistake, however, of only a slightly different order than the would-be poem's, to reduce Mariani's work to a recapture or modern-day rendition of a bygone sensibility. While the author's prodigious familiarity with the myths and literature, with the geography and history of Greece and Rome, inform his work in a way that has led one critic "to associate *Il torto della preda* with Aristophanes, as parody and philosophy both affirm and cancel one another in an exercise of reciprocal vitality" (Davide Bracaglia, POESIA, 97, summer 1996), there are as well, throughout Mariani's oeuvre, undeniable echoes of an ancestry that comprises Seneca and Job, Belli and Montale, Vallejo and Ritsos. What Mariani shares with all of these presences —in both the severe and diamond-sharp incisiveness of some poems, as well as in the swirling baroque richness of others— is the classical ideal of poetry as a medium, if not of truth, of truthfulness. It is an ideal, I would suggest, that for all of its "conservative" aspirations still merits space in a literary marketplace where faddishness is often confused with originality, and recognition trades places with accomplishment. It is an ideal, moreover, that in Bracaglia's words, in making room for "a mixture of the trivial and the sublime, paradoxically earmarks Mariani as a contemporary poet and a *critic* of classicism." Or, as the highly regarded critic Emilio Zucchi writes, in a review of *Il torto della preda* (*Gazzetta di Parma*, Feb. 10, 1996): "In Mariani one finds a poetry of the word as bread, bread broken and shared, kneaded from the idea that truth must, must, must exist in the form of a common language. As the poet admonishes in a verse of his: *'Non c'è conchiglia / che rifaccia il vero / verso del mare'* [No shell / can sound the veritable / verse of the sea]."

In sum, the passionate intelligence and lyrical "nobility" of Lucio Mariani's verse earmark him—in my estimation—as a poet highly worthy of being rendered in English. Within a lyrically saturated culture such as ours, infused with the kind of celebration of the ego that characterizes so much confessional poetry, Mariani's verse points to both difference and need. His work, in fact, restores to the lyric—through images both dense and porous, lines both cadenced and spasmodic—an ancestral, mythical sensibility that reminds us of our place in history *today*, at the start of a dizzying and displacing millennium. It is a poetry that re-claims for itself a centering and ethical function—which is different, say, than a denouncing or moralizing one. (Nowhere is this fact better evidenced than in the somber, dignified verses of "Checkmate," Mariani's hymn commemorating the lives lost in New York's twin towers on September 11, 2001.) Along these lines, in reading Mariani, one is reminded of the quality embod-ied by the likes of Eugenio Montale, or William Meredith: poets whose elevated but subdued tones, in celebrating the *pietas* and *pathos* of our condition, everywhere betray a defining commit-ment to a timeless human capacity for both integrity *and* doubt. Few voices today sing in such a way as to combine successfully ele-gance and "courage," music and "wisdom." Thus inspired, Mari-ani's voice does; and it is in this sense that I believe his poetry to be—far from outdated, or nostalgic—important, timely, and in-deed essential.

*

A few closing words. While most of the references in the book—cultural, historical, and literary—are readily traced, there were a few deemed in need of clarification. For this reason I include at the end of the volume a page of brief notes. Throughout, titles originally in languages other than Italian have been maintained. I should also note that while *Echoes of Memory* presents most of the poems originally collected in *Il torto della preda*, it is rounded out by a small selection from the poet's most recent volume, *Qualche notizia del tempo* (Some News of Time), published in 2001. In sum, then, this volume documents a prodigious career of more than twenty-five years and bridging four decades, dat-ing back to the 1970s.

Many people, needless to say, have made this effort possible across time and space. The poet's own thanks are extended to his foremost Italian publishers, Milan's Crocetti Editore and Rome's Edizioni dell'Elefante. Personally, I am grateful to the editors of several noteworthy U.S. journals—*Pequod, Alea,* and

Literary Imagination—where prior versions of some of these translations first appeared. The American Academy in Rome, especially in the person of its former director Caroline Bruzelius, was instrumental in fostering a connection with Mariani. As the connection has since developed into a deep and honored friendship —and not only with the poet but his family as well—I am doubly indebted to Caroline for her gift. Special thanks go to Thomas Harrison, both for his afterword and the delicate precision with which he read and helped fine-tune my translations. (It was also Tom's broader reading of Mariani's poetry, and his emphasis on "remoteness," that led to my choice of the title *Echoes of Memory.*) Enzo Crea, Caroline Howard, Fred Feirstein, Kevin Z. Moore, and Paul Feinberg also contributed, all in significant ways, toward completion of the project. I thank them too for their help and support.

Anthony Molino

L'ancora e l'amo in fondo fanno parte
dello stesso infissibile discorso.
Dal tempo verde al tempo perigeo
la sosta dura quanto la pastura
la pastura non dura che l'avvento
della nuova occasione e la speranza
indovina guadagni differenti
come per magistero naturale.
Lo stanziale è altra bestia. Per lui
l'amo talvolta e l'ancora comunque
son superfetazioni.

The anchor and the hook are at bottom
part of a single, selfsame discourse.
From prime to perigee
the stay lasts as long as the grazing
the grazing lasts but the advent
of a new occasion, while hope
fancies earnings of another sort
as if by its very nature.
Who stays put is a different beast. For him,
the hook, at times, and the anchor
always, are superfetations.

Accade
di onnidire in un baleno
solo a se stesso
e quando
un lume aggiorna
sulla liturgia.

Alone with oneself
one happens
to allsay in a flash
and just when
a light dawns
on the liturgy.

L'ETERNITÀ

a Luca

Mentre l'eternità figlio,
l'eternità è quel modo di te
che ho potuto donarti stabilmente
un tralcio sotterrato
nel parco dei tuoi umori
che riaffiora nel sorriso improvviso
nell'inabilità della mano a sfabbricare
nella curiosità che ti dà il mare
forte e continua più della paura
nel rispettare il misero antropino
nell'amore del vino e delle poppe.
Eterna figlio è la tua parte
eterno quel milligrammo mio
che domani ed insieme ingombreranno
il gesto della scimmia tua devota
qualunque sia
per sangue o suggestione. E così via.

ETERNITY

for Luca

Whereas eternity, my son,
eternity is that way of yours
I managed indelibly to bestow
a brier hidden
in the garden of your moods
that sprouts in your sudden smile
in your hand's inability to craft
in the curiosity the sea inspires
stronger and steadier than any fear
in your respect for the lowly little man
in your love for wine and tits.
Eternal, my son, is the part of you
eternal that milligram of mine
that tomorrow together will burden
the gesture
of any and every monkey to you devoted
whether by blood or influence. And so on.

Sono tornato all'isola dei venti
dove svetta e governa fra i gerani
il girasole.

Dove la canna inarca lance al meltemi
che fa calva la rocca
e scala al mare, farneticando
fra rovigli bruni fra bruni grilli
e brune lagartiglie
in concerto di fasci sibilanti sulla battigia,
tentativi di turbine
poi mille costure all'acqua.

Strappa il cielo una nuvola.
Il bavero del vecchio caicco
si gonfia è un fico maturo,
vola come un messaggio verso Delo
porta sacra del divino intervallo.
Qui una regola di civiltà pietosa
non consentiva nascita né morte.

Laggiú tra le sedie cresciute sulla spiaggia
Chatzidakis piange la sorte del postino
con tutte le corde delle correnti di mare.

Si scorda dove porta la strada

I've returned to the island of winds
where the sunflower towers and lords
                    over geraniums.

Where the meltemi bends reeds into lances
balds the rock
and slopes to the sea, raving
amid brownish shrubs, brownish crickets
and brownish lizards
in a concert of whooshes along the shore
efforts at whirlpools
that break into endless crests.

A cloud rips the sky.
The old caique's collar
swells, is a ripe fig,
soars like a message toward Delos
sacred gate of the divine interval.
Here a rule of merciful law
admitted neither birth nor death.

Down below, amid chairs spawned on the beach
Katzidakis cries the mailman's fate
with all the chords in the currents of the sea

Forgetful of where the road leads

Luna velina come una pastiglia
di menta consumata,
contro i muri di spugna
le falci delle rondini crudeli
incrociano stridendo.
La sorpresa di un gelso, la gramigna
e tigi indistinguibili
profughi semi
fra le scaglie dei tetti
immobilissime.

Vigila il freddo
all'alba.

Moon sheer as a fading
mint
sickles of cruel screeching swallows
crosscut
the spongy walls.
The surprise of a mulberry tree, weeds
imperceptible stems
refugee seeds
amid stilled
slivers of rooftops.

At dawn
the cold keeps watch.

Mi chiedi d'esser l'altro che comprendi,
quello che parla lentamente, chiaro,
che descrive le piazze partendo dai negozi
che del mare
discute il salino, il rischio, la grandezza
che lasci la sera
ritrovi il mattino inalterato.
Mi chiedi d'esser l'altro
che cadenza la cura
dell'orto e del tuo frutto
acqua per l'acqua
fronte per la fronte
che morde con i denti
e il giorno divide dalla notte,
non cerca indizi di luna.
Mi chiedi d'esser l'altro
che conosce per nome
i suoi nemici e il giusto
che non lima un dubbio rotondo
che sputa le spine del ventre
che lo scriccio di foglia calpestata
chiama rumore.

Mi chiedi d'esser biondo.

You ask me to be the other you comprehend,
the one who speaks slowly, clearly,
who describes a piazza from its shops
and discusses the sea's
salinity, its risk and grandeur
whom at night you leave
to find in the morning, unchanged.
You ask me to be the other
who cadences the care
of your garden and fruit
water for water
brow for brow
who bites with his teeth
to divide night from day,
indifferent to the moods of the moon.
You ask me to be the other
who knows what's right
and his enemies by name,
who smooths the edges of doubt
and spits up the thorns in his gut,
who calls the crackle of a leaf underfoot
noise.

You ask me to be blond.

Adesso
con che segno
risponderai al silenzio?
C'è rischio che ritorni
la fregola di fare
tutto
di trovare due nuove bandierine
e agitarle per dire che va bene
di seguire la mosca e il funerale
contemporaneamente
di baciarci a natale
di tornare alle corse sospesi
sopra tutti i possibili vuoti
di scordare che questo è il silenzio
che succede alla mossa,
unico ragionevole risparmio
fra i suoni
i suoni
le combinazioni.

Now
through what sign
will you respond to the silence?
The risk is that the itch
to do it all
will return
to dig up two new pennants
and signal that things are fine
to follow the fly and the funeral
both
to swap kisses at Christmas
to return to the races suspended
over every conceivable void
to forget that this is the silence
that follows a chess move
the only sensible saving
amid the sounds
the sounds
the combinations.

Notte di ferro, emula forma
della mia stanchezza, noi non balliamo più.
Rimetto a posto i panni
con le dita di chi va accumulando
ordine e sonno. E le bandiere
volano ridendo verso tetti lontani.

Night of iron, emulous form
of my fatigue, we dance no more.
I put away my clothes
with the fingers of one who collects
order and sleep. And the flags
flutter laughing at faraway rooftops.

Avere uno stile
così sbaratto vino per bottiglia
le prime placche induriscono il segno
e comincio a morire
ma li avrò tutti un po' rassicurati.
Non avere uno stile
come il corallo in ramo
mantenere le ciglia rivolte
oltre le opposte nuvole del tempo
e ammettermi accidente, costringere
gli altri a rifare continuamente i conti
visto che vivo per chiamate di immagini
e non penso, non penso.

To have a style
and swap wine for a bottle
early symptoms harden the mark
and I start to die
not without reassuring them all.
To not have a style
like coral on a branch
to turn one's gaze
beyond the opposing clouds of time
and admit being an accident, to force
the rest to continually take stock
since I live at the beck and call of images
and never think, never think.

LETTERA
per Carlotta

Non è facile, amata
portare a spalla il cerchio dell'assenza
tra le marche gualcite di tabacco
e dischi crocefissi
e non è buono
masticare l'aspro vuoto
che offende stanze più magre
copre l'annuncio magico dei fiori
m'invade occhi e ragione come un grido.
Non è facile, amata
diradare le foglie del silenzio
e travedere il caracollo del mio stambecco
quando chiude la corsa sorridente
ritornato alla valle longobarda fra bricconieri
che attendono alla posta dietro il grasso songino.
Lo so, lo so che al mare nasce più raro
il cespo ed impervio difficile a strappare
lo so, lo so che in branco la paura si svende
e il tiglio del consenso accarezza i tuoi sogni
lo so, lo so che i figli chiedono pane
e più chiedono carne.
Non è facile, amata
farti capire con le mani e gli occhi
che qui si può svernare per la vita
dove t'amiamo in due, il luccio ancora bravo
e il tuo poeta nei quaranta brandelli
in due definitivi come i giri del tronco.
Non è facile, amata
rivelarti perché nessun delitto
ha fatto un morto solo.

LETTER

for Carlotta

It's not easy, my love
to shoulder the circle of absence
amid crumpled cigar labels
and crucified LPs
and it's not good
to chew on the acrid emptiness
that offends emaciated rooms
covers the magic that flowers announce
invades my eyes and mind like a scream.
It's not easy, my love
to thumb through the leaves of silence
and glimpse the gambol of my wild goat,
its run over, smiling, home again
in its Longobard valley among poachers
in ambush behind the blackberry.
I know, I know that bushes are rarely
born by the sea, and hard to uproot
I know, I know that fear comes cheap among the horde
and that berries of harmony caress your dreams
I know, I know that when the children ask for bread
what they're asking for is flesh.
It's not easy, my love
for my hands and eyes to make you understand
that here we can spend the winter for life
where two of us will love you, the spry jackfish
and your forty-something poet in tatters
the two of us definitive like the rings of a tree trunk.
It's not easy, my love
to reveal you, for never did a crime
claim only one victim.

Rari giorni d'inverno quando la tramontana
spezza gli aliti al fiume e tende il cielo
come se contrappunto fosse il Giura e invece sono
queste martoriate pietre che bussano ai lastrici
divini, la sola porta impropria perché a Roma
non spettano salvezze.
Cosí dicono gli orli delle case, fratturati
cristalli d'arabia, trapunti dalle luci e dai suoni mattini,
lo dicono fumando i meccanici topi
e i natali non soffici né sacri, anche lo dicono
le sue morti feriali, la mia coperta corta.
Lo ripetono qui—minimamente—
i cerini di lusso che s'accendono a stento
fra le mani di chi non ha più fede
nell'avvento di un nuovo nord. In questi rari
giorni d'inverno quando il sole mi pesa così poco
sarà bene tenere alta la testa. Forse si vive altrove.

END OF DECEMBER

Rare days of winter, when the north wind
snaps the river's whiffs and stretches the sky
as if the Jura were its counterpoint; still,
it's these tortured stones that knock at the divine
ceiling, the one wrong door, for Rome
can lay no claim to salvation.
So say the frames of houses, their cracked
Arabian crystals, pierced by morning lights and sounds,
so say the smoking mechanical rats,
the Christmases, neither gentle nor holy, and so say
its weekday deaths, and my blanket, all-too-short.
And so here insist—faintly—
the stylish matches lit with difficulty
by the hands of who no longer trusts
in the advent of a new north. In these rare
days of winter, when the sun weighs so lightly upon me,
it is wise to hold one's head high. Life perhaps is elsewhere.

Meridiana domenica, il sole
arruola paccottiglie di suoni millenari,
dico sedie, campane, figli in fuga
tintinni d'un'incudine flemmatica,
dalle finestre le voci di giornali domestici.
E il borgo è dissepolto.
Grave un fianco del Campidoglio protende
speroni e fichidindia insaziabili di luce.
Tra scaglie di cioccolato infranto
il gatto dichiara pace al mondo ad occhi chiusi
come moneta rovesciato sulle margherite.

Noontide, on the Lord's day, and the sun
recruits trinkets of age-old sounds,
I mean chairs, bells, children in flight
the clinks of an indolent anvil,
from windows voices of domestic chronicles.
And the neighborhood is unearthed.
From a towering flank of the Campidoglio
spurs and prickly pears devour the light.
Amid chocolaty slivers of tufa
a cat, eyes closed, declares peace
to the world, like a coin flipped over in the daisies.

In libertà, dicevi, conta la microregola
è come un altro mondo dal quale
vorrei poter tornare.
E intanto ferma e dolce
mi inforcavi i capelli insaponati
mi stendevi la pelle con quale mestiere
e io là nello stesso abbandono
del cane grattato sulla groppa
pensavo a quanti laccioli, alle benizie
che la manutenzione dell'amore
infiora.

In freedom, you'd say, what matters are the microrules
it's like another world where
I want to be able to return.
Meanwhile, steady and gentle,
you raked my soapy hair
expertly stretched my skin
and me, mellow as a dog
whose back's been stroked,
I'd think of all the snares, the niceties
strewn by the upkeep
of love.

A dispetto del mentore
la vita non si scrive in stampatello.
È in clinato corsivo, corsivo accidentato
virgole, macchie, late esitazioni
un solo punto fermo.
Nell'impero dispotico del bianco
qualche sorriso incanta.

To a mentor's dismay
life is not set out in print.
It scripts itself, in clines, along an obstacle course
of commas, stains, marginal hesitations
one lone fixed endpoint.
In the despotic empire of the blank page,
smiles are sometimes enchanting.

Qua sotto, dove il carrubo lavora ombra
grasso imperlando ninnoli caduchi
qui devi abbassare tutto
timbri registri penne parola
scendere insomma dal trespolo ventoso
beccucciare a terra e riempire la gola secca
di canzonette.

Senti poco lontano gli scherzi verdi del mare.

THE CAROB

Down here, where the lavish carob kneads
shade empearling ephemeral trinkets
here you must drop all
signets, accounts, pens, the word
descend, in short, from the windy perch
peck at the earth and fill your parched throat
with jingles.

Not far off you hear
the green joshing of the sea.

Quella notte d'estate frinita di grilli
la luna interloquì disapparendo
tra le nubi costiere e subitanea
depose un'ombra nera dall'orto fino a noi.
Nella pozza del buio la tua parola
si ruppe e naufragò come una barca
di carta, colta dal sasso
d'un monito insensato.
Mai più a lungo serrasti le mie dita.

SHIPWRECK

On that summer night chirping with crickets
the moon cut in, and disappeared
behind coastal clouds, wasting no time
to shroud us and the garden in shadow.
In that puddle of darkness your voice
broke, shipwrecked
like a paper boat against the rocks
of a senseless admonition.
Never again did you clasp my fingers.

Errore blu
prendere nella rete
tutti i rumori
che pungono la vita.
Ad esempio, la nenia
la fitta nenia delle mosche non è
né utile né gaia.

WARNING

Blue mistake
to net
all the noises
that sting life.
For example, the buzz
the thick buzz of flies
is neither useful nor gay.

ASSENZE

Doveva essere un mese molto distante da aprile.
Agli occhi non approdavano rondini né il loro ricordo,
tre dita scrivevano in aria glifi gentili
preghiere d'un ostaggio al nume intermittente.
Niente accusava di vita la pallida ghiaia
lo sconosciuto respiro
i pantaloni di marmo appesi sul filo infinito.

ABSENCES

It must have been a month far removed from April.
Neither sparrows nor their memory alighted before my eyes.
Three fingers inscribed gracious glyphs in the air,
prayers of a hostage to an intermittent god.
And no accusations of life were levied
against the drab pebbles, the unfamiliar breath,
the stone trousers dangling from the infinite clothesline.

D'inverno se pensi a una barca
e non sei marinaio
la vedi passare irta di bianche velerie
ai piedi d'un cielo stupefatto
sola e distante come una sposa disabitata
che il muto gabbiano accompagna
attraverso gli spazi d'un fondale di scena
dove l'onda non frange
né acqua così turchina potrà mai bagnarti.

Niente ritorna
e ogni barca che passa è perduta.

Tu non sei marinaio
prova a Natale
se mento.

In winter, if you think of a boat
and aren't a sailor
you see a bristling white canvass adrift
at the foot of a dumbfounded sky
alone faraway like a deserted bride
whom the mute seagull accompanies
across the backdrop of a stage
through spaces where no wave ever breaks
and never will turquoise waters spray you.

Nothing returns
and every boat that passes is lost.

You're no sailor
try proving me wrong
at Christmas.

Dopo
dopo che avrai imparato
a dividere il plurale dei fiori con un colpo
di ciglia
dopo che avrai pesato ogni silenzio
sul pianto della vite crocifissa
e sulla fame del tarlo
dopo aver visto
negli occhi d'una volpe pellegrina
che sorrisi spietati fa la luna
dopo
si dovrebbe tentare la città.

Oppure arrivarci dal mare,
arse le notti di vento attraversate
sull'altalena fra le aguglie e orione
spento il deliquio nella sontuosa sera di bonaccia.

Ah la maledizione di un poeta urbano
apprendista di astrazioni e di gatti!

After
only after
you'll have learned
to split the plural of flowers
with the beat of an eyelash
after you'll have weighed every silence
on the tears of the crucified vine or
upon the woodworm's hunger
after seeing
in the eyes of a pilgrim fox
what vicious smiles the moon can make
only then
should one make for the city.

Or get there by sea
across parched nights of wind
on a swing arching between spires and Orion
swooning no longer in the sumptuous lull of evening.

Ah, the curse of an urban poet
apprenticed to abstractions and cats!

AUSPICIO

Ah Marta, mia garbata tenerezza
dovrebbe capitare una frattura
con tanto di squassi
una separazione grande nella vicenda
della contiguità continuità
—tu che cominci dove io finisco
stipite e porta l'uno all'altro inastati
o piuttosto trasfusi e irreperibili come
nell'usato composto verbale—dovrebbe
capitare di staccarci
non dico per sempre ma
solo il tempo che basta
ad estinguere i prestiti reciproci
e ritrovare passi discordi
bersagli e dentifrici personali
sintassi di due perse solitudini.
Insomma Marta, rivorrei le mie ossa
per un po'.

Oh, Martha, my sweet, my grace
it would take a fracture
a thunderous upheaval
a tearing asunder of our
contiguity our continuity
—you who begin where I end
closet and door unto each other hoisted
or, as if transfused and lost
in an oft-used compound word—but
what if we take a break
not forever but just
time enough
to extinguish our debts with one another
and learn again to step out of sync
find our own targets and toothpaste
the syntax of two lost solitudes.
Basically, Martha, I'd like back my bones
for a while.

CONSOLATORIA A MARTA

> *Make me thy lyre, even as the forest is:*
> *What if my leaves are falling like its own!*
>
> P. B. Shelley

Non ti dolere se le favole nuove
slittano sul cervello e se ne vanno
volando come le rosse foglie di novembre
che s'acquetano nelle forre invisibili e nei fossi.
Non è, non sarà male perché ogni storia
conclude la sua fuga dentro i porti del vento
e resterà paziente ad aspettare il nostro arrivo
lieve.

CONSOLING MARTHA

Make me thy lyre, even as the forest is:
What if my leaves are falling like its own!

P. B. Shelley

Grieve not if today's fairy tales
slide off the brain and flutter
away like red leaves in November
to settle in ditches and invisible gullies.
No, it's no grievous loss, for each story
ends its flight in the harbors of the wind
and there patiently awaits
our soft arrival.

Ho imparato a salutare affabile la morte
nella camelia nera dove tace la mente.
E non parlo dell'anima, anzi
dell'anima è da dire la partita
felice.

*

Camelia nera, camelia dalle spire di miele
che fuoco infligge l'incendio dei tuoi petali
come immaga quella bocca minoica di insidie
quale dolce canzone nei gorgogli del morbido marese.
A un cenno della luna le mie mille colombe
partono per cercare la via che arriva al cuore
e, smarrite, s'affondano a morire nelle gore
del tuo segreto regno.

I've learned to greet death amiably
in the black camellia where minds hush.
Nor do I speak of the soul
of the soul whose happy demise
I otherwise sing.

*

O black camellia, honey-ringed camellia,
what flames do your petals' fire inflict
how luring the menace of your Minoan mouth
how winsome the song of your sweet swamp!
At a nod of the moon my thousand doves
fly off to find the road to your heart
but, lost, they plunge to their death
in the ditches of your secret realm.

Mi piace vederti spalancare
tutte le bocche di fuoco
dilatate, fumanti, aizzando
farmi scegliere in quale anfrattuosa spira
seppellire l'imbroglio.

I want to see you open wide
your every mouth of fire
dilated, smoking, goading
me on to choose in which tortuous nook
to bury the hoax.

Vorrei usare con te
che di me usi invita,
fino ad ascosíe abissali e
ghiacci le mie salive come vetro
soffiato alle pareti del respiro,
quando passi e ti spacci
da intangibile diva ma rasenti
gli sguardi presenti caracollando
tartarica e opulenta sull'eccesso
dei fianchi.
Salvi chi può la mente
io
mi schiaccio al muro, mi faccio
grillo silente,
le antenne immote nell'ideogramma
di resa
che ti ostini a ignorare,
segnano V come vinto.

I'd like to engage you
you who unwittingly engage me
through to the abysses of my being
and ice my saliva like glass
blown against the walls of my breath
when you walk by and make
like some untouchable diva grazing
the gazes of bystanders
with the opulent, Tartarian bounce
of your bountiful hips.
While others may salvage their minds
I'll
crush my back to the wall and become
a silent cricket
my antennae stilled in the ideogram
of surrender
you so obstinately ignore,
that signal V, for vanquished.

MACCHIA IL CAMPO

Guarda là il papavero impudico continua
a falleggiare nelle spighe ritrose rubescendo.
Come un ospite senza invito fatta strada in un lampo
si prende libertà innominabili sotto il lenzuolo
che trepida verde a un soffio rafficante,
macchia il campo di fuoco.
Il cardillo svezzato da poco
frizza gli occhi e s'infuga.

Look, how the impudent poppy reddens still
pricking its way through reticent wheatfields
taking, with the zip of an uninvited guest,
unspeakable liberties under the sheets
that tremble greenly in the blustery breeze,
staining the field with fire.
The goldfinch, just weaned,
squints and scurries off.

Se conto bene
il seme di Platone dista dal mio soltanto
ottantasei madri di madri e un po' di fortuna.
Gli evi sono festini di famiglia, ma rovesciate
in bocca alla tv le ultime gocce di assoluto
l'anima frulla flebile
come una nottola colpita al radar
batte contro astutissimi vantaggi
perde velluto e piomba nel vespaio dei cinici.
Presto i suoi resti saranno il pulviscolo vago
che l'onda del sole
solleva nel vuoto maligno.

If my calculations are correct
Plato's seed is removed from mine only
eighty-six mothers of mothers and a bit of luck.
Eras are family whoopees, but once the TV
slurps up the last drops of transcendence
the soul flutters feebly
like a bat stripped of its radar
crashes into the shrewdest of ratings
and, no longer velvety, plummets into a trap of cynics.
Soon its remains will be specks of dust
that waves of sun
stir in the malignant void.

Sanguinando, sanguendo
entra di spalla dalla porta socchiusa
vecchio cane bianco
gli occhi chiedono scusa
di avere perso proprio l'ultima volta
allegria e guerra.
Conviene a zanne di ventura
alla natura di libero bastardo
atterrare sul fianco ai bordi del comò
e muto guardando l'angolo lontano
andarsene pudico.

DOG'S DEATH

Bleeding, bloodied
nudging the door with its shoulder
the old white dog enters
eyes that say sorry
for having lost, for the last time
war and whimsy.
It's good that fangs of fortune
that bastards born free
should land on their side by a night table
and, staring in silence at the far corner,
bashfully take their leave.

Quante volte ti sono morto a fianco
—quasi altrettante risorto—e ti accorgi di me
soltanto adesso mentre cammino i fiordi
ricamati dall'ultimo geranio, la gola tesa
ai pubblici pugnali.

Accreditare l'anima fra le mura di casa
pretende saggi di azzurre funambolie:
ombre dei martiri miei, soccorrete da Mileto e da Elea!

How many times have I died by your side
—for nearly as many resurrections—yet you notice me
only now, as I walk the fjords
laced by the last geranium, my throat tendered
to public daggers.

To enhance the soul amid one's own walls
calls for the skills of sky-blue acrobatics:
shades of my martyrs, hasten to my aid from Miletus and Elea!

a Egon Schiele

Un grappolo di corvi balla sui nodi del platano
neri raschiano l'aria taluno planando cordialmente
fino al Goethe affondato nella poltrona di bronzo.
Ah Schillerplatz Schillerplatz, neanche il tempo
per sentire freddo perché all'accademia
mettono in vista cento gocce di sangue
mani chiodi occhi grida e un figlio abbandonato
sulla calce, tutto a precipitare nel mistero vermiglio
della carne spaccata, quel ventre che sorride
come la bocca d'un sicario paziente
dietro gli ossi e le spine.
Una dopo l'altra ecco spiegate le ragioni
per non attendere ancora.
Egon, povero Egon quando un bambino è solo
anche la febbre è rimedio.

VIENNA, FEBRUARY 29
for Egon Schiele

A cluster of crows dances on the gnarls of the sycamore
black, they rasp the air, an off-one gliding gleefully
round Goethe sunken in his armchair of bronze.
Oh, Schillerplatz Schillerplatz, no time even
to feel cold for at the Academy
a hundred drops of blood are on display
hands nails eyes shrieks and a son left
in a white hole, everything crashes in the crimson mystery
of quartered flesh, a womb that smiles
like the mouth of a hitman, patient
behind the bones and thorns.
One by one these are the reasons
to wait no longer.
Egon, poor Egon, for a child alone
even a fever is a remedy.

Adele ama secche le foglie e i fiori
ama l'anima secca.
Adele è una vela di sangue rappreso
che geme al fiato del minimo vento
al sussurro, al più pallido accento d'umana ventura
ogni voce la piega, dolente.
Adele cammina spedita
sul filo di lana delle incantate aporie
che giorno per giorno cattura e difende
senza chiedere aiuto
parlando paziente ai miti feticci di casa
guardando attraverso
le cose e i vestiti che incontra per strada.
Ho visto Adele alle prese con una mondanità sola
ogni mattina domanda il cappuccino e un croissant,
queste dolcezze per lei si chiamano vita.

Adele loves dried leaves and flowers,
loves the dry soul.
Adele is a sail of clotted blood
who quivers at the slightest whiff of air,
at a whisper, at the faintest accent of human misfortune,
who, at the sound of a voice, doubles over.
Adele walks hastily
along a tightrope of charmed double binds
that day by day she captures and defends
asking no help
in patient talk with meek household fetishes
oblivious
to the objects and dresses she meets on the street.
I've seen Adele grapple with a single worldly pursuit
ask every morning for a capuccino and croissant.
Such is the sweetness she calls life.

SPIAGGIA DI SETTEMBRE

Condite sirene, nostre signore in trono
fra palette e gomitoli fanno prove dal vivo
e per l'intero giorno
va in onda il passaggio del mestiere
a frotte guazzanti di apprendiste.

Nel malvato imbrunire ancora volteggiano
minacce a catena e schiaffi artigianali
occhiate che colpiscono al cranio
i calvi padri assorti ad altra carne, imprendibile.

Non c'è conchiglia
che rifaccia il vero
verso del mare.

SEPTEMBER BEACH

Spiced-up sirens our ladies, enthroned
amid shovels and needlework, busy
rehearsing for the day-long live broadcast
of the profession's bestowal
upon throngs of splashing apprentices.

In the mauvish dusk threat after threat still dips
and circles as do crafted slaps
and glances that strike the skulls
of bald fathers intent on other flesh.

No shell
can sound the veritable
verse of the sea.

ERLEBNIS

a Marzia

Figlia, non fare come me
che non mi lavo i denti per fumare di più.
I guasti meno lievi della morte
si possono evitare.

ERLEBNIS

for Marzia

Daughter, don't be like me, who
to smoke more doesn't brush his teeth.
Mishaps lesser than death
can be avoided.

A te penso
uomo di Tenerife
qualsiasi mulatto sui cinquanta
che stai girando l'angolo e dietro al chiosco
pisci di buon umore sul muro polveroso
mentre ritorni a casa, alla casa di latta
avvolta nel benevolo dicembre
uomo di Tenerife
ti sto guardando
io che non esisto per te
dentro nessuna stanza della terra
né posso somigliare a un profilo
della nuvola vaga
a te penso comunque
fratello immaginario e al fatto
che mai più sentirò la tua corsa
oltre il baleno
di questa evocazione solitaria
in una fredda notte d'Europa
penso a te nato forse nel mio giorno
che senza pena senza meraviglia
nello stesso mio giorno
morirai.

I'm thinking of you
man from Tenerife
of any half-breed in his fifties
as you turn the corner and behind the kiosk
piss heartily against the crumbled wall
as you go home, to your four walls of tin
wrapped in this benevolent December
man from Tenerife
I look at you
I who don't exist for you
in any room on earth
nor can I resemble the outline
of a vague cloud
and yet I think of you
imaginary brother and of the fact
that never again will I sense your course
beyond the flicker
of this solitary evocation
on a cold night in Europe
I think of you born perhaps on my same day
stranger to pain and wonder
you who on my same day
will die.

Finalmente come un platano urbano
cresciuto a furia di pisciar dei cani
utile e triste.

At last like a city tree
sprung by the ruthless pissing of dogs:
beneficial and glum.

Una mattina
arriverò a tenere fra le mani
l'immagine tua, le dita di filo
il sorriso, la morte di eroe ferito.
Oggi ancora ti fingo
un'esclamazione sommessa,
di fronte ai quaderni
non muovo silenzio per trattenere
amore.
Nel vuoto un genio t'accompagna
ti posa in un piatto di sabbia
scivolo alla larga
vorrei lasciarti per ultima
così ho fatto sempre
con la castagna più dolce.

One morning
I will manage to hold in my hands
the image of you, the threadlike fingers,
your smile and wounded hero's death.
Still today I pretend
you're a hushed exclamation,
face my notebooks
and shuffle no silence to sustain
love.
In the void a genie accompanies you
rests you in a tray of sand
I slip aside
to keep you for last
as I always did
with the sweetest chestnut.

EFESO

I

A tre ore dall'alba, ancora stenta il sole a farsi varco
tra i pini di Aleppo, estatici guardiani del silenzio.
Efeso è qui come una spora rosa lasciata sul pendio
da venti etèsi, scompaginata nello sciatto volo.
Efeso è qui vedova delle spume, un'esule di mare nelle spire
limose del piccolo Meandro, qui confitta e arenata
méndica il ventre antico di sponda estrema che accolse
Egeo nel disperato salto. Efeso è qui, memore di tramonti
convertiti nel bagliore di aurore occidentali,
quando dal porto le donne ionie vedevano salpare
intemerati i remieri di Focea e spargevano in acqua
le corone intrecciate con le foglie di vite e i gelsomini.

continua

I

Three hours since daybreak, and still the sun struggles to pierce
the pines of Aleppo, ecstatic guardians of silence.
Ephesus is here, like a pink spore left on the slope
by Etesian winds, ruffled in its random flight.
Ephesus is here, widow of foaming seas, exile of waves mired
in the spirals of the lesser Maeander, here, riveted, shipwrecked
imploring the far-off ancient shore that embosomed Aegeus
in his desperate leap. Ephesus is here, mindful of sunsets
recast in the dazzling glow of western dawns,
when Ionian women watched from the harbor
as the intrepid oarsmen of Phocaea set sail, and decked the water
with wreaths braided from grape leaves and jasmine.

continued

II

Per questa terra abrasa i nostri occhi di cane
rovistano i gomitoli del tempo, tutte le età rapprese
nelle vene delle colonne morse, lungo il petalo bruno
d'una cavea sonora, tra i nomi consumati sulla pallida
stele abbandonata all'abbraccio di oliastri. Battiamo
i piedi dove rovescia il furore dei Cimmeri, dove
la Grande Madre versa seme di toro e lacrime dell'ape,
dove sgorga il discorso di Eraclito, un rivolo di fuoco
e di lapilli che scavalca i millenni e con le spine
e gli ossi del frammento ancora frusta di misteri la mente,
battiamo i piedi dove ripara Antonio a regalare
l'ultimo sorriso ai satiri e alle menadi.

continua

II

Across this abraded land these dog eyes of ours
scour the strands of time, the ages curdling
in the veins of gnawed columns, the sallow petal
of a clanging cavea, the names consumed on an ashen
stele abandoned to the embrace of oleasters. Our feet
tread there where the fury of the Cimmerians pounds, where
the Great Mother spills the seed of bulls and tears of bees,
where the word of Heraclitus gushes, stream of fire
and lapilli hurdling the millennia, fragments of thorn
and bone that still now scourge the mind with mysteries.
Our feet tread there where Antony takes refuge
to offer one final smile to the satyrs and maenads.

continued

III

Né il crocidio del corvo infrange il cielo né un pendolo
suadente di cicale. La via che sale e la via che scende
sono una sola e la stessa. Come fiori di marmo
dalle mille stagioni ininterrotte, ali di testimoni
corteggiano la strada dei Cureti e il passo che la solca,
vita e morte confuse nella formula immobile del tempo. Allora,
queste nostre ombre sottili sono anche l'ombra di coloro
che spesero il destino per i secoli d'Efeso la Grande e nella luce
ora sorgono e sono. Al fondo del cammino, alte le fiamme
della devozione, brucia per sempre la biblioteca di Celso
e nel rogo lo scheletro solenne della pietra apre un mirario
che racconta agli dei la storia d'una dedica filiale,
avventura interdetta agli immortali, onore degli umani.

III

Neither the cawing crow nor a swaying pendulum
of cicadas shatters the sky. The way up and the way down
are one and the same. Like marble flowers
of a thousand uninterrupted seasons, wings of witnesses
court the road of the Curetes and our own fresh tracks,
life and death confused in the quiescent formula of time. Thus,
these wiry shadows of ours are also the shades of those
who spent their destiny for the centuries of Ephesus the Great,
who in the light now rise, and are. At the end of the road, amid
towering flames of devotion, burns forever the library of Celsus
and in the blaze the solemn skeleton of stone opens a spiracle
to tell the gods a story of filial homage,
an adventure denied the immortals, a solely human honor.

Da Venezia non furono commerci
ma grandi operazioni di marea.
Spinsero piazze e ottagoni di fonte
ai piedi di Minosse; ne resero
la canzone d'oriente che ogni notte
affonda nelle calli
rivive il giorno dall'oro frantumato
tra le labbra degli angeli
che assentono morendo.

What hailed from Venice wasn't trade
but vast transactions of tides.
Pushed were piazzas and octagons of fountains
before Minos; in return
for a song of the Orient that nightly
plunges through the *calli*
and relives by day in the cracked gold
of the lips of angels
who dying nod their assent.

I piedi leggeri sul selciato
sanno sfiorare i brividi d'un lago
come soffi obliqui al vortice.
Cosí passano indenni i poeti
dai portici alla piazza
le tasche gonfie di guanti da sfida
avvolta l'anima deforme
nelle carte gualcite, nei giornali,
il naso è una prua che s'impenna
sull'arte del sorriso ignorato.
Da giocatori di superfluità
conoscono a memoria
le regole del vuoto.

Feet light on the pavement
they know how to graze the quivers of a lake
like breezes oblique to the eddy.
And so do poets pass unharmed
from the porticos to the square
their pockets bulging with gauntlets
their deformed souls wrapped
in crumpled pages, in newspapers,
their noses prows upturned
on the art of a smile ignored.
Players of superfluousness
they know by heart
the rules of the void.

Nessuno oltre i cespugli dello stupore,
oltre la forma ironica del guscio.
E più nessuno arriva a portare notizie
degli oracoli. Sulla riva muschiata degli stagni
lungo i viali di ghiaia
dai monti dolci come seni innevati
tutto il presepe marcia sul posto,
le valige vuote, senz'ombra, senza sguardo,
sotto la trama delle stelle appese al soffitto di carta.
Né sorride per noi bianca la luna.

CRÈCHE

No one beyond the hedges of wonder,
beyond the ironic form of the shell.
No one comes anymore with word
of the oracles. On the mossy banks of ponds
along pebbly roads
down mountains soft as snow-capped breasts
the entire crèche marches in place
casting no shadows, bundles and gazes empty,
beneath the plot of stars dangling from a cardboard ceiling.
Nor does the white moon smile upon us.

MIELE

Dacché sembra finito il tempo nostro,
in questa sciarra ignobile conviene
lasciare campo all'assiolo e all'astore.
Per difendere il sogno sul filo del millennio
il grande esperimento consisterà nel solo
sottrarci, nell'opera in levare
versando fondi d'anima a pochi degustatori
goccia per goccia, come miele estremo.

HONEY

Since our time appears to be over
it makes sense in this muck and mayhem
to clear the way for the owl and goshawk.
To defend the dream at millennium's end
the grand experiment will consist
solely in stepping aside, in muting tones
decanting extracts of soul for a few select tasters
drop by drop, the rarest of honeys.

Quando fu certo che gli indizi di esistere non bastano
e niente serve alla vita quanto un testimone,
provvide il cielo che ogni uomo avesse
un logografo al seguito. Ma le storie cantarono
súbito e solamente di acrobati divini
perché, mortali o no, tutti i furieri
sono sempre uguali. A noi, rimase l'ombra.

QUARTERMASTERS

When it was clear that clues of being aren't enough
and nothing benefits life more than a witness,
the heavens decreed that every man
should have his own logographer. But what got sung
were only and always tales of divine acrobats
since, mortal or not, quartermasters are all the same.
We, we were left with shadows.

Superba maga della solitudine,
quarantanni rasente la vita senza
toccarla, ogni sera nascondevi una mano
ferita nel grembo, ogni sera. La morte
—non una luce rossa aveva lampeggiato
non avvisi di commiato—con quella
hai fatto centro al primo colpo,
solo il tempo di raccogliere le rose
bianche, gli iris dei pochi astanti storditi
e poi via, in polvere, sotto bossi e viburni
d'una valle montana che un suono mite
di campana desolava.

Proud sorceress of solitude
forty years brushing never
touching life, hiding, night after night
a wounded hand in your lap. Death
—not a single red light flashed
no hint of a farewell—that
you got right the first time,
in time only to gather the white
roses, the irises of a few stunned bystanders
and off you were, dust, under the boxwoods
and snowberries of a mountain valley
made desolate by a churchbell's meek ring.

Le donne muoiono d'autunno nel minimo clamore
quando qualunque amore è consumato. Ne sono garanti
le date incise in tutti i camposanti di monte e di mare.
Appena si fanno deserte di voci le stanze, le donne
sono certe che altra attesa non serve a intercettare
l'avvenire e alle prime luci d'autunno si staccano
dal cuore come foglie di gelso. Cadono docili sul fondo
nell'isolato annuncio di giornale, le presidiano
sillabe discrete di compianto.
Basta il più tenue vento.

Women die in autumn, in a hush,
when any love is long consumed. Just check the dates
chiseled in mountain and seaside graveyards.
No sooner do voices desert the rooms than women
know no further waiting is needed to intercept
other seasons, and like mulberry leaves
they loosen from their hearts. And they flutter
to the bottom of a far-off obituary, guarded
by discreet syllables of grief.
The slightest of winds is enough.

Tu mi guidi solerte e non vedi fra i campi
che la falce di luglio ha mutato il fasto dei poggi
in groppe bionde di sauri sorpresi al galoppo.
Nell'aria salda di tramonto e cicale
taste di fieno scalano il fianco dei colli
assediano il cipresso indulgente al sommo
come tamburi e cumuli di scudi abbandonati.
Quasi i resti d'una giostra indetta dall'estate
al tessere dei merli e delle bigie
sembra conclusa adesso la battaglia leggendaria
per celebrare in un encausto d'oro la fine
dei grandi scannamenti cantati dalla storia
e dall'arte a Montaperti, Anghiari, San Romano,
Monteriggioni, e via glorie dicendo.
Allora corri fuori, verso le rughe dei calanchi calvi
corriamo miti a malve musicali. E che Haydn ci assista!

CONCERT-GOING, ORCIA VALLEY

Eager, you guide me but don't see across the fields
that July's sickle has turned the kingly knolls
into a golden gallop of startled steeds.
In this poised air of sunsets and cicadas
haycocks climb the hillslopes
where, like drums and heaps of abandoned shields,
remains of a summer joust,
they lay siege to a lenient cypress.
In a weave of blackbirds and chariots
the legendary battle now seems over
so as to celebrate in a gilded encaustic
the end of the grand massacres sung by history
and art: Montaperti, Anghiari, San Romano,
Monteriggioni, and so on, glory after glory.
So run now, make for the wrinkles in the bald ridge
let us run meekly toward musical mallows. And may Haydn help us!

LETE

a Valerio Magrelli

Giorno o notte, all'ora indefinita
quando viene alla vita un verso grande,
una poesia vera, fosse per caso
fosse invenzione d'un nemico in arte

devi comprare una cravatta rossa
e vestirti di lino come si faceva
nella festa di Dio. Dopo leverai dalla testa
il cappello con garbo per dire all'oblio

che questa volta non potrà masticarti
né il suo coltello avrà oggi altra carne
se a tutti è nato un nuovo figlio immortale.

E nell'andarne, prendi una viola e gettala
ai flutti opachi del Lete. Avrà perduto ancora
per una gioia che non scorderai.

LETHE

for Valerio Magrelli

Day or night, at that indefinite hour
when a solemn verse comes to life,
a true poem, whether by chance
or through the invention of an enemy in art

you need to purchase a red tie
and put on a linen suit, as was the custom
for the Lord's feast. With grace, then,
you will tip your hat, to convey to Oblivion

that this time he'll not devour you
nor will his knife exact other flesh
for a new immortal child has been born unto all.

And as you leave, take a violet and cast it
into the opaque pools of Lethe. Who will have lost
yet again, for a joy you will not forget.

Dicono che si scriva sempre la stessa poesia
come l'acque d'altura fiottano getti immutati
come la cerva batte el mismo camino sulla neve
salvo impercettibili scarti di sospetto,
salvo un grave allarme che detta nuovi alfabeti della resa
e fa piangere a ognuno il suo poema.

They say it's always the same poem that gets written
The way highland waters spray selfsame streams
The way a doe treks *el mismo camino* in the snow
If not for the imperceptible sidesteps of suspicion
If not for the grave alarm that sounds new alphabets of surrender
And prompts each of us to cry the poem that is ours alone.

Parla sempre meno
sempre meno.

Rima del limpido silenzio.

Se poi i connoisseurs de l'âme
sono esauriti (il diavolo li fotta)
le velette non servono
e di modiste infatti neanche l'ombra.

Cantare il meglio del nulla—o il peggio,
è lo stesso—non è un buon mestiere.
Ogni rumore, ogni avvento dopo la curva
d'un giorno affoga nei raggiri del ricordo
e tu a stare lì sul ciglio riflessivo, all'erta
per altre ferraglie e per l'incidente del pane
mentre in mano ti cresce la mano di tuo figlio
finché non potrai più sentirla.
Intanto
spoglio pioppo gelso nodoso abete
diventano cinque parole buone a interdire
l'assalto del sonno.
Ci vuole legna diversa per riscaldarsi un po'
in attesa che passi l'assoluto.

*

continua

Talking always less,
always less.

Rhyme of clear silence.

If then the connoisseurs *de l'âme*
are all used up (may the devil screw them)
veils serve no purpose:
of milliners, in fact, there is no trace.

To sing the best of nothingness—or the worst,
same difference—is no trade to ply.
Every noise, every advent around the bend
of a day drowns in the wiles of memory
and you, there, on the thoughtful verge, made vigilant
by clanking noises and the question of bread
while the hand of your son grows in yours
until you'll feel it no longer.
In the meantime,
barren poplar mulberry knotty fir
become five words good to head off
the onslaught of sleep.
It'll take another kind of wood to get warm
while waiting for the Absolute to pass.

*

continued

Allora versami parole come gocce
minime quiete
questi nidi di voce
disfatti in sussurro.

Il mondo finisce ogni notte
stagnano incenso e fragole
ma una luna non basta.

Ora riassunti
in polvere si può volare
noi
materia di passeri e comete.

La passeggiata è finita.
Si imbarcano nel cielo
i fogli dei quaderni abbandonati
sotto l'ulivo poso la memoria
come un cappello inutile
sento
le operazioni del silenzio
attraversare il cuore.

*

continua

So pour me words like minimal
quiet droplets
these voice-nests
unpacked in a murmur.

The world ends every night
incense and strawberries linger
but one moon is not enough.

Now summed up
in dust we can fly
we
the matter of sparrows and comets.

The stroll is over.
The pages of abandoned notebooks
board ship in the sky.
Beneath the olive tree I lay down my memory
like a useless hat
feel
the workings of silence
across my heart.

*

continued

È dissolta
la nuvola dei giorni.
L'odore di mimosa prende
la stanza alla gola.
Lo dovete sfilare dolcemente
con due dita
per posarlo sull'acqua
e cancellare l'ultimo messaggio:
farsi catturare viva
è l'unico torto della preda.

Dissolved
is the cloud of days.
The scent of mimosa grabs
the room by the throat.
Unstring it gently
with two fingers
to lay it on the water
and erase the final message:
getting captured alive
is the prey's lone mistake.

Sono nato a Rockaway, sotto Brooklyn, in un lembo
di terra che sembra un dito largo e teso nell'Atlantico.
Non ricordo donna che m'abbia custodito d'amore
l'infanzia e i primi incanti. Ma è stato bello crescere
dietro una siepe, ogni giorno l'oceano negli occhi, bello
come scovare orgoglio malnascosto nella faccia italiana
di mio padre la volta in cui entrai a casa con il primo
stipendio da contabile. Volle giocare una partita a scacchi
e fumando due sole sigarette, fece che lo battessi senza scuse
su una mossa di torre e di regina. Concluse che dovevo
sempre stare attento alle torri, comunque infide nei loro
movimenti lunghi su un percorso di croce bianco e nero.

"Infide", disse serio il mio vecchio e ricordavo la parola
sorridendo di martedì quell'undici settembre mentre correvo
a lavorare per Manhattan.
                          E il suo monito posso riconoscere
ora che sono polvere dispersa da un lampo osceno
polvere abbandonata fra altre polveri scomposte sotto
un marciapiede divelto, a fianco della foglia dove
mio padre non potrà mai trovarmi nemmeno
per tenermi la mano degli scacchi. Ero di Rockaway
e non ho avuto amore né conforto di donna:
una adesso ne venga e chieda agli iris bianchi
di fiorire nel nome mio indistinto, cancellato.

Roma, 26 settembre 2001

CHECKMATE

I was born in Rockaway, below Brooklyn, on a strip
of land that looks like a fat finger stretching into the Atlantic.
I remember no woman who cherished my cradle or teenage
awe. And yet, it was special to grow up behind a hedge,
with the ocean every day in my eyes, special
to uncover the pride my father's Italian face couldn't hide
the time I brought home my first paycheck as a CPA.
He wanted to play chess and, smoking but two cigarettes,
let me beat him unequivocally, on a combination rook-and-queen.
He ended by saying to always watch out for those treacherous towers
and the black-and-white crosses their long moves plot.

"Treacherous," he said, somberly: I remembered the word
with a smile that Tuesday, September 11,
as I raced to work through Manhattan.
                    And I recall his warning now
that I am dust scattered by an obscene blast
dust lost among the dusts of others undone
below a ravaged sidewalk, next to the leaf where
never will my father find me not even
to hold the hand I'd use to play chess. I came from Rockaway
where I knew no woman's love or warmth:
may she now come and ask the white irises
to bloom in my name, faded, erased.

Rome, September 26, 2001

Lucio Mariani: The Remoteness of Poetry

Beyond linguistic experimentation and the fashioning of new idioms for thought, poetry is an art of remoteness. It arises from the distance between speaking and living, between one thing and another just beside it, from the very foreignness of the voice to the air that it fills. Remoteness is harbored in lives long passed and others unborn, coursing through the blood like a "milligram" of sameness transmitted from father to son (as in Mariani's poem "Eternity"). It even speaks from beneath the rubble of the devastated towers in Manhattan ("Checkmate"). Remoteness measures degrees of absence, which may be the covert foundations of presence, proximity and union.

Lucio Mariani is a supreme poet of remoteness. The spur to his lyrics is usually no more than an occasion—a mere *occasio* that happens to befall, like a current of wind or a dawn in Rome. Many such occasions are tinged with loss, signaling the death of a dog, the end of a romance, or a historical splendor in ruins. Others speak of distance between people: father and daughter, lover and other, poet and stranger. All hint at the reasons and motivations of poetry—tense points of contact, unrecognized links, the impulse toward communion. Thus, in "Coincidences," an anonymous passerby takes on the guise of a strange species of twin, perhaps born the same day as the author and destined to die the same day as well. A lacuna is registered and filled.

Other occasions bring the repressed to the surface, as in "September Beach," where matronly housewives, decked out as "spiced-up sirens," in Molino's adroit formulation, cast furtive "glances that strike the skulls / of bald fathers intent on other flesh." The phrasing also shows how carefully Mariani captures other remote echoes in the occasion's substructure—players in a quite different poem, Stéphane Mallarmé's "L'Après-midi d'un faune," along with the sirens that elicit the inaugural "Salut" of Mallarmé's own collection. The outcome, in this and other poems, is a dense, terse, and allusive construction, folded into numerous layers of reference, phonetically and semantically packed.

Does no *sententia*, no sharp message, emerge from these ambiguous, occasional relations? One does, but in the way that a tree thrusts out of a concrete sidewalk, nourished by the ruthless "pissing of dogs." If we ponder the title of the poem built on this image ("Faire part," invitation to participate), we see that Mariani wants us to assess consequences by their cause. Something like the experience of this tree, he suggests, may underlie all belonging, participation, and group commitment. Origins must be tallied with outcomes.

This contextualizing operation is typical of Mariani's writing. It restores origins and outcomes to the mute event. "Tarpeian Rock," for example, focalizes imperial Rome's conversion from paganism to Christianity in the term *domenica*, the "day of the Lord." On the Sunday in question, in a much changed Rome, poetry, with the rousing power of the sun, "recruits" acoustic trumpery as old as the millennia—bells, anvils, and the sounds of "children in flight." Clearly, the sounds do not occupy the same ontological plane; but they waft through a single, vastly dilated time. What seems to have passed is still present. As these disparate sensations are gathered, *il borgo è dissepolto*, "the neighborhood is unearthed." We witness a resuscitation, one all the more welcome in view of the original function of the Tarpeian Rock— a stage for ancient executions. Things live through poetry—in the occasions exhumed by poetry—by being *dissepolti*, unburied from the contemporary scene. Poetry uncovers and reverses those deaths, eventually grafting them onto the image of a cat sunning itself in peace.

Remoteness is not only what is pondered in poetic reflection; it is the "fact" to which poetry responds. After all, if poetry had nothing to summon or draw near, it would have no reason for being. Its harmonies are evoked by dissonance, resolved in some cases by Aristotle's essence of the poetic (metaphor), in others by the fabulous synesthesias of the symbolists or the syntactical fusions of the surrealists. In each instance, poetry undoes the suppressions of present-mindedness, the habitual equation of the actual with the real. It harkens to the remote. If the results appear less constructive in our time than in earlier generations, it is probably because contemporary poetry has so much more working against it, including a cultural animus toward that pensive leisure from which poetry springs. For some years now, poets have thought their mission best approached by a negative act, one underscoring the very need for poetry and stipulating what conditions best serve this need. That, in fact, is a recurring motif of Mariani's graceful, ironic, noble verses: transcendence of the present and reconciliation with the distant are goals more pressing than ever, politically no less than metaphysically. They may even be the secret project of each living occasion; and, as such, require the poet.

With "feet light on the pavement," Mariani's poets are breaths barely grazing the "quivers of a lake" ("Poets"). Intimate with "the rules of the void," they excel in the "superfluous," or what overflows each defining container. Despite their best efforts to provoke a duel, they have little effect on social action, passing unharmed from portico to square. What is it, then, that lifts the prow of their poetic vessel? According to this poem it is the wave of a smile disregarded. Is this the smile of the poet, condescending to those denying life's deep contentions? Or is it an emblem of vague, intuited unions? In either case poetry gauges the difference between full and empty hands, in line with that strong Italian tradition linking Petrarch and Leopardi to Ungaretti and Montale.

Remoteness is harbored in time and culture. It calls for archaeological excavation, a critique of tradition. Like *Janus bifrons*, Mariani the Roman has double vision, looking forward and backward, perceiving gain in the loss and loss in the gain. "If my calculations are correct," begin his wry and learned lines on Plato's *Timaeus*, "Plato's seed is removed from mine only / eighty-six mothers of mothers and a bit of luck." The word for luck, *For-*

tuna, also names the deity convulsing the millennia between one writer and the other. True, Mariani minimizes the gap in this fantasy of common mothers; but what do his reckonings show? That in the current age the "last drops of transcendence" ooze into and out of the TV set, while, standing helplessly by, "the soul flutters feebly": *L'anima frulla flebile.* Even these words have their remote echo, invoking the famous flight of the soul in the emperor Hadrian's "Animula vagula blandula."

It is no surprise that Mariani mines sacred plots of the West for his topics: the assaulted towers of New York City; Mikonos, the gateway to Apollo's holy Delos; the gleeful apocalypse of Vienna, figured by Egon Schiele; the ancient city of Ephesus, where the poet finds the conflagration of the Celsius library still raging. All of it marks an exorbitant consumption of historical memory. Hometown to the philosopher Heraclitus, Ephesus means tragedy and paradox: "mindful of sunsets / recast in the dazzling glow of western dawns." Why not recall, too, that "the way up and the way down / are one and the same"? The line stands as both motto and justification for Mariani's recuperative enterprise. Indeed, for a poet seeking to undo the destructions wreaked by time, the paradox becomes an article of faith. In the cultural sum total, "these wiry shadows of ours are also the shades of those / who spent their destiny for the centuries of Ephesus the Great, / who in the light now rise, and are." Poetry again serves as a vehicle for resurrection, driven against Fortune by the spirit of humanism, buoyed by the powers of invocation and recollection. And this is an operation of the lyric in one of the highest senses of the word, forging its bonds in extraordinary euphonies, in semantic discoveries and conceptual relays. Poetry, for Mariani, is a gesture of "filial homage," perhaps even the sole "human honor" one can render those forgotten by time. If there is to be any spiritual continuum, it must be built on the provisions of poetry, on counters of identification, on the very foundations of communication (a word that in more remote times, of course, meant "making common").

Twisting the conventional meaning of a Mariani title, we might say that the *tempus tacendi*—the time of silence—is the only *tempus loquendi*—the time for speech. In the current realm of the counterepiphanic, the main task is to reference what the present lacks. The fiery and ironic pathos of Mariani's later poems lends the poet the role of an "enemy in art" ("Lethe"), a martyr of destiny's forgetfulness, no different from the victims of sacked Miletus, birthplace of Thales, Anaximander, and Anaximenes, or from those of the sophist Zeno's Elea. Lightfooted or grave, the poet has no choice but to "enhance the soul amid one's own walls."

In fact, by the end of this bold collection, Mariani invokes the muses much less than he does those who take a stand against "alphabets of surrender," or codes of intellectual oblivion. His lines speak on behalf of *nidi disfatti in sussurro,* "voice-nests unpacked in a murmur." Where other poets may be wont to celebrate "divine acrobats," Mariani remembers ignored quartermasters. He prefers sounding out spaces beneath those we ordinarily inhabit, in a poetry echoing its cultural ambition. By the end of his poetic trajectory, spanning a period of thirty years, the self-ironizing distance marking the early poems, all enveloped in a wry and noble acquiescence, has given way to an urgent and combative spirit, one alarmed, after all, by the remoteness to which poetry is wedded.

Thomas Harrison

P. 4 *Tempus tacendi tempus loquendi:* This Latin phrase, an echo of Ecclesiastes ("a time to hush, a time to speak"), is inscribed on a Renaissance tomb of the distinguished Malatesta family in Rimini.

P. 25 *Tarpeian Rock:* Named after Tarpeia, who betrayed the citadel to the Sabines and was killed by them, the Tarpeian Rock is the precipitous face of Rome's Capitoline Hill, believed to have been the place where traitors were executed. (Source: G. Masson, *The Companion Guide to Rome.*)

P. 35 *Warning:* In Italian elementary schools, teachers traditionally corrected students' work by highlighting serious mistakes in blue pencil. Lesser mistakes were underlined in red.

P. 59 *Elea:* A small town in Southern Italy known today as Velia, it was one of the ancient Magna Graecia colonies known for having welcomed the philosophers Xenophanes, Parmenides, and Zeno.

P. 66 *Erlebnis:* The term is German, for "experience."

P. 70 *Faire part:* The term is French, akin to a "public announcement"; literally, to invite participation.

P. 95 *Concert-Going, Orcia Valley:* The places and events cited refer to historic, blood-soaked battles fought on Tuscan soil and celebrated in famous works of art. Among these, Montaperti (1260) was the site of a battle between Florence's Guelphs and Ghibellines, of which Dante writes in cantos 10 and 32 of the *Inferno.* (The poet also writes of Monteriggioni, a Sienese outpost in the city's war against Florence, in canto 31.) Anghiari (1440), commemorated in Leonardo's magnificent "Studies," saw the militia of Milan's Visconti family pitted against the joint forces of Florence and the pope. Finally, San Romano (1433), a costly defeat of Siena at the hands of Florence, is exalted in three marvelous works by Paolo Uccello, housed in London's National Gallery, the Uffizi, and the Louvre.

P. 107 *Checkmate:* This poem was written in the wake of the September 11, 2001, terrorist attack on New York's World Trade Center.

LUCIO MARIANI was born in 1936 in Rome, where he now lives. He is the author of eight volumes of poetry: *Antropino* (Padova: Rebellato, 1974); *Ombudsman ed altro* (Milan: Guanda, 1976); *Panni e Bandiere* (Rome: Il Pruno, 1980); *Bestie segrete* (Milan: Crocetti, 1987); *Dispersi gli alleati* (Milan: Crocetti, 1990); *Pandemia* (Rome: Edizioni dell'Elefante, 1990, under the pen name "Astro Falisco"); the book of selected poems *Il torto della preda* (Milan: Crocetti, 1995); and *Qualche notizia del tempo* (Milan: Crocetti, 2001). Mariani's cyclical poem *Del tempo* (Rome: Edizioni dell'Elefante, 1998), presented at Coimbra's Biblioteca Joanina, has been translated in France and Portugal. His poems have appeared in all of Italy's major poetry journals and have been translated and published in Greece, the United States, Spain, and France. Mariani has translated into Italian the *Songs of Priapus* (Florence: Ponte alle Grazie, 1992), as well as works by César Vallejo, Tristan Corbière, B. M. Koltès, J. P. Velly, Rosanna Warren, and Yves Bonnefoy. His other writings include the volume of essays and aphorisms *In bassa sapienza* (Rome: Edizioni dell'Elefante, 1991); the play *Trono del buio* (Milan: Crocetti, 1993); and a collection of short stories entitled *La notte di Misso Flegià* (Rome: Empiria, 2000). In 2001, under the auspices of the University of Rome, a multilingual volume entitled *Lucio Mariani, poeta per l'Europa* (A Poet for Europe) was published to honor the poet and his work.

ANTHONY MOLINO is a widely published psychoanalyst and literary translator, as well as general editor of Wesleyan's *Disseminations: Psychoanalysis in Contexts* series. He began his career as a translator while on a Fulbright scholarship to the University of Florence in 1980. Since then he has won three grants from the Pennsylvania Council on the Arts, major fellowships from the Academy of American Poets and the National Theater Translation Fund, and a 1997 affiliate fellowship with the American

Academy in Rome. His translations include Antonio Porta's *Kisses from Another Dream* (City Lights Books, 1987), *Melusine* (Guernica Editions, 1992) and *Dreams and Other Infidelities* (Xenos Books, 1999); Valerio Magrelli's *Nearsights* (Graywolf Press, 1991) and *The Contagion of Matter* (Holmes & Meier, 2000); as well as two plays: Eduardo De Filippo's *The Nativity Scene* (with Paul Feinberg: Guernica, 1997; also anthologized in *Twentieth-Century Italian Drama: The First Fifty Years*, Columbia University Press, 1995), and Manlio Santanelli's *Emergency Exit* (with Jane House, Xenos Books, 2000). Molino lives with his wife and son in Italy.

THOMAS HARRISON is professor of Italian at the University of California, Los Angeles, where he teaches twentieth-century literature, aesthetics, and film. He is also the editor and translator of *The Favorite Malice: Ontology and Reference in Contemporary Italian Poetry* (Out of London Press, 1983), author of numerous articles on modern Italian poetry (Zanzotto, Ungaretti, Montale, D'Annunzio, Leopardi), and author of a study of expressionism in poetry, music, painting, and philosophy titled *1910: The Emancipation of Dissonance* (University of California Press, 1996). In 1992 he published *Essayism: Conrad, Musil and Pirandello* (Johns Hopkins University Press).

2 801